Countries of the World

South Africa

Virginia Mace

Kate Rowntree and Vukile Khumalo, Consultants

NATIONAL GEOGRAPHIC

WASHINGTON, D.C.

Contents

Foreword

South Africans welcomed the 21st century as citizens of a young democratic country. In 1994, South Africa had held its first full election in which all South Africans could vote. The outcome of the elections was a new form of government that accommodated all the people of South Africa. The party that received the lion's share of the votes was the African National Congress (ANC). The ANC leader, Nelson Mandela, had served more than 20 years in prison, and now he had become president with the task of forming a government of national unity. This new government is guided by a constitution that embraces human rights and the dignity of all citizens.

The new republic was embraced by the family of nations—the United Nations. South Africa's reception internationally brought hope after the years of isolation caused by the apartheid laws. These laws had separated South Africans according to the color of their skin. Today's South Africa is a powerful force and a voice of reason in Africa and the world.

While South Africa sees itself as a young democracy, it also draws from its long history that dates back to prehistoric times. Thanks to recent discoveries in archaeology, South Africa is home to some of the earliest human remains ever found. For this reason, South Africans like to refer to their land as the "Cradle of Humankind."

But South Africans also recognize the importance of more recent history, especially the last 200 years. In that time modern Africa was created, with economies based on minerals and other natural resources. These events have had more effect on today's South Africa than any others. The mining industry alone transformed people's lives in the 20th century and continues to shape the future of South Africa.

At the heart of South Africa's vibrant economy and political system are diverse and rich cultures. As the political changes swept through South Africa in the 1990s, a new musical sound called *kwaito* also emerged in the townships of South Africa. The music drew from all the country's cultures and languages and offered something very original to the lives of South Africans.

▲ A lioness babysits the cubs while the other members of the pride are off hunting. South Africa has one of the largest populations of wild lions in the world.

Vukile Khumalo
University of KwaZulu-Natal

A Land
Without
Equals

YOU CAN SEE THE SHAPE of Table Mountain from miles away. When the southeast wind blows, a "tablecloth" of white cloud covers the top of the mountain and spills down the sides. According to legend, a pirate named Van Hunks was smoking a pipe on the ridge between Table Mountain and neighboring Devil's Peak. The devil challenged him to a smoking contest; the prize would be Van Hunks' soul. The contest has gone on ever since, creating the clouds that roll over the mountain.

On clear days the mountain top offers spectacular views. Visitors can hike to the top or take the easy route—a 10-minute ride by cable car. The car spins around slowly so every passenger gets a chance to see in all directions across the city of Cape Town below.

◀ The flat top of Table Mountain is shrouded in cloud as it stands high above the busy city and harbor of Cape Town.

WHAT'S THE WEATHER LIKE?

I n general South Africa has a sunny climate. Most areas receive rain in summer. However, a lot of the country is dry and faces water shortages at other times of year. The east gets the most rainfall and the west the least. The map opposite shows the physical features of South Africa. Labels on this map and on similar maps throughout this book identify most of the places pictured in each chapter.

Fast Facts

OFFICIAL NAME: Republic of South Africa

FORM OF GOVERNMENT: Republic

CAPITAL: Pretoria (Tshwane) (administrative), Cape Town (legislative), Bloemfontein (judicial)

POPULATION: 47,400,000

OFFICIAL LANGUAGES: Afrikaans, English, IsiNdebele, IsiXhosa, IsiZulu, Northern Sotho, Sesotho, Setswana, SiSwati, Tshivenda, Xitsonga

MONETARY UNIT: rand

AREA: 470,693 square miles (1,219,089 square kilometers)

BORDERING NATIONS: Botswana, Lesotho, Mozambique, Namibia, Swaziland, Zimbabwe

HIGHEST POINT: Njesuthi 11,181 feet (3,408 meters)

LOWEST POINT: Atlantic Ocean—sea level, 0 feet (0 meters)

MAJOR MOUNTAIN RANGE: Drakensberg

MAJOR RIVERS: Limpopo, Orange

Average Temperature & Rainfall

Average High/Low Temperatures; Yearly Rainfall

JOHANNESBURG: 77° F (25° C) / 42° F (5° C); 28 in (72 cm)

UPINGTON: 94° F (35° C) / 35° F (1° C); 7 in (19 cm)

DURBAN: 82° F (28° C) / 51° F (10° C); 42 in (105 cm)

SUTHERLAND: 81° F (27° C) / 27° F (-3° C); 9 in (24 cm)

CAPE TOWN: 79° F (26° C) / 45° F (7° C); 24 in (61 cm)

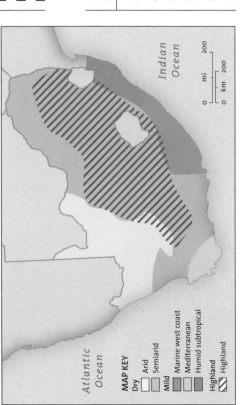

Atlantic Ocean

Indian Ocean

MAP KEY

Dry
- Arid
- Semiarid

Mild
- Marine west coast
- Mediterranean
- Humid subtropical

Highland
- Highland

0 mi 200
0 km 200

MOZAMBIQUE

TROPIC OF CAPRICORN

ZIMBABWE

Limpopo

Soutpansberg

BUSHVELD

BLYDE CANYON, page 11

Blyde River Canyon

SWAZILAND

SUBURBS, page 15

Witwatersrand

Crocodile

Pretoria (Tshwane)

Johannesburg

Vaal

Vaal Dam

Njesuthi 11,181 ft 3,408 m
(Highest point in South Africa)

GOLDEN GATE, page 10

Tugela

D R A K E N S B E R G

LESOTHO

Richards Bay

Pietermaritzburg

Durban

LESOTHAN BOYS, page 12

SOUTH

Bloemfontein

Orange

Gariep Dam

Stormberg

Bambes

Great Fish

Suurberg

East London

Port Elizabeth

AFRICA

H I G H V E L D

Sneeuberg

Valley of Desolation

Molopo

BOTSWANA

KALAHARI DESERT

NAMIBIA

Orange

AUGRABIES FALLS, page 14

Upington

Augrabies Falls

Groot Vloer

Great Karoo

Nuweveld

FOSSIL SKULL, page 11

Roggeveld

Komsberg

Sutherland

Little Karoo

Cape Town

Table Mt.

BEACH HOUSES, page 15

Saldanha Bay

Olifants

Kamiesberg

Port Nolloth

Orange

Walker Bay

Cape of Good Hope

Cape Agulhas

TABLE MOUNTAIN, pages 2, 6-7

CAPE OF GOOD HOPE, page 13

Atlantic Ocean

Indian Ocean

Africa

Indian Ocean

Atlantic Ocean

SOUTH AFRICA

MAP KEY

⍟ National capital

● Selected city

□ Site

+ Elevation

miles 0   200

km 0   200

▲ The Golden Gate Highlands National Park is one of the most scenic parts of South Africa's central plateau. It is an area of sandstone cliffs and caves located in the Free State.

The High Plateau

Two-thirds of South Africa is plateau—high, flat areas. It is highest in the east, reaching 8,000 feet (2,440 m) around Lesotho and dropping to 2,000 feet (610 m) in the Kalahari Desert in the west. The rolling grasslands that cover much of the plateau are called the Highveld. Bushveld—tree-dotted plains—covers the rest.

The weather on most of the plateau is pleasant— it seldom gets too hot or cold. Rain comes in thundery downpours during summer. The exception is in the south where the plateau forms dry areas called the Great and the Little Karoo.

Beneath the surface, the plateau has vast resources of gold, uranium, and other minerals, especially close to the Vaal River. As a result, the industrial heartland of the country, Witwatersrand, is located there.

DRY DESOLATION

The Valley of Desolation in the Eastern Cape was formed over millions of years as heat, cold, and water caused the rocks to crumble, forming bizarre shapes and imposing pillars that rise 400 feet (120 m) above the seemingly endless plains of the Great Karoo. *Karoo* is a Khoikhoi word that means "the land of thirst." Although the Karoo is not a desert it is still dry. It rains only a few times each year. The grassy landscape is broken by steep-sided, flat-topped hills called *kopjes* (*kah-pee*). In the past few people lived in the dry Karoo. Today thousands of wind-powered pumps draw up groundwater to supply communities and farms.

▲ The skull of a dinogorgon—a giant hunter older than the dinosaurs—lies on the dry plain of the Great Karoo.

The Great Escarpment

The Great Escarpment is an almost continuous chain of mountain ranges that encircles the plateau on the east, south, and west. Along its eastern length it is called the Drakensberg—Dragon's Mountain. To the west, the mountains go by other names, such as the Stormberg, Bamboes, and Sneeuberg.

The Drakensberg range is 700 miles (1,225 km) long and rises to more than 11,400 feet (3,475 m). Dutch settlers named the range for the legend of

▼ The Blyde River flows through a steep-sided canyon that forms part of the Great Escarpment. The Blyde River Canyon is the third largest in the world.

a dragon, which had its den deep in the mountains. The Zulu name Ukhahlamba, meaning "barrier of pointed spears," is a better description of the sharp peaks that rise above the steep eastern slopes. The mountains are tall enough to be covered in snow for a few weeks in winter.

Opposite Coasts

Durban on the east coast and Port Nolloth on the west coast lie on almost the same line of latitude. That means that both cities are the same distance south from the Equator. However, Durban is much warmer than Port Nolloth—an average of 11° F (6° C) warmer. Durban and the rest of KwaZulu-Natal on the east

A COUNTRY WITHIN A COUNTRY

Nestled in the Drakensberg Mountains, on the edge of the Great Escarpment, is the little kingdom of Lesotho. It shares a border with South Africa, but that border goes around in a circle—Lesotho is completely surrounded by its neighbor. It was founded in the 1800s by a chief called Mshweshwe who hid from an army of Zulus in the hills. He united small groups to form the Sotho nation. Britain took over Sotho in 1868, renaming it Basutoland. In 1966 that became independent Lesotho. The mountain kingdom is the source of much of South Africa's river water, and its huge Katze Dam supplies its neighbor with electricity.

▲ Lesothan boys stand above the Great Escarpment on the frontier with South Africa.

coast are warmed by the Agulhas Current, which flows south from the hot tropics. Tourists bask on long, sandy beaches and tropical crops such as mangoes, pawpaws, litchis, bananas, avocado pears, and sugarcane grow in the region. That gives KwaZulu-Natal its popular name of the Garden Province. Summers are hot and humid with heavy rain showers.

Cold and Dry

The western shores are cooled by the Benguela Current, which flows northward from the icy Southern Ocean around Antarctica. The current is filled with the minerals used by tiny marine plants and animals called plankton. Masses of plankton, known as blooms, make the west coast a rich feeding ground for small fish, such as pilchards and anchovies.

The western coastal land is much less fertile. The cold ocean current does not bring much wet weather with it, so the land is dry for much of the year. Instead of rain, fog and low clouds are common.

TRAVELING HOPEFULLY

In 1488 Portuguese explorer Bartolomeu Dias saw a rocky headland at the southern tip of Africa. According to legend Dias named it the Cape of Storms. However the king of Portugal renamed it the Cape of Good Hope because it marked the gateway to the Indian Ocean and the riches of India and the East. The Cape is not the most southerly point in Africa (that honor lies with Cape Agulhas further east). However, it was the most important point for sailors because of the violent storms in the area. Ships preferred to pass the Cape on a sunny, windless day, but howling gales and pounding seas were more typical of these waters. Legend has it that the sea giant Adamastor haunts the waters of the Cape, taking vengeance on anyone who dares to disturb him.

▼ The Cape of Good Hope is at the very tip of the Cape Peninsula, a strip of land than runs south of Cape Town.

River Systems

South Africa has two main river systems: the Orange and the Limpopo. The Limpopo River begins as the Crocodile River in the Witwatersand Mountains in the north of South Africa. It then arcs east to form the country's northern border before flowing into the Indian Ocean via Mozambique.

▲ A quarter of all of South Africa's water runs through the Orange River and over the mighty Augrabies Falls.

The Orange River is the longest in South Africa and carries more water than the Limpopo. It rises in Lesotho and flows westward to the Atlantic Ocean. The river supplies the farms of the Northern Cape with much need water. In the middle of the dry plain, the wide river plunges through the steep granite walls of a ravine in a series of rapids and waterfalls. One of the falls—the Augrabies Falls—is considered to be one of the world's greatest. It tumbles 625 feet (191 m) to a deep pool surrounded on three sides by rocky walls. According to legend the deep pool contains a fortune in diamonds that have been washed down by the river through the centuries.

Contrasting Cities

South Africa's cities have very different personalities. Johannesburg, or Jo'berg as South Africans call it, is

South Africa's city of business, and everyone is busy and frequently on the move. About 12 miles (20 km) southwest of Johannesburg is the sprawling district of Soweto. It was built as a township—a place to house black laborers—so the center of Johannesburg could be reserved for white people. Today Soweto is a vibrant place and sets trends in music and dance.

Durban is South Africa's beach city. The beaches tempt its residents to sunbathe, surf, or stroll around the yacht basin. Cape Town is South Africa's city of culture with a cosmopolitan heritage of Dutch, French, British, and Malaysian influences. Its vibrant waterfront provides the backdrop for an everchanging mixture of musicians and performers. Pretoria, South Africa's administrative capital, has always been a quiet city. It is called the Jacaranda City because of the purple blossomed-trees that line its streets in spring.

▲ Luxury apartments line the beaches of the Cape Peninsula, beneath the cloud-capped Twelve Apostles hills.

▼ The neat suburbs of Johannesburg spread out from the central districts of apartment buildings and offices.

From
Aardvark
to
Zebra

MAGINE TRYING TO CATCH a two-ton (1.8 tonnes) rhinoceros that can charge at 25 miles (40 km) an hour. First you fire a tranquilizing dart into the rhino. Once the animal has gone to sleep, you blindfold it and attach ropes to its horn. Then you inject an antidote to the drugs inside its ear. It works so quickly that you must dash for safety as the rhino staggers to its feet. Your team pulls on the rope and guides the dozy rhino into a crate. In the 1960s this dangerous work was the only way to save South Africa's white rhinos. Rhinos were being hunted for their horns and faced extinction. Operation Rhino changed all that. 3,500 white rhinos were captured and moved to safe areas in South Africa and around the world. Today there are 5,000 white rhinoceroses in South Africa.

◄ The white rhinoceros is actually gray. Its name comes from the Dutch word "weit," meaning wide, a reference to its square muzzle.

PROTECTING WILDLIFE

The map opposite shows South Africa's main vegetation zones, or what grows where. These vegetation zones, or ecosystems include savanna, grassland, semidesert, forest, desert, and fynbos (fain-bos), a zone named after a group of evergreen plants with small, hard leaves that grow there.

South Africa founded its first national park, Kruger National Park, in 1926. In 1994 the government set a goal of increasing protected land from 5 to 8 percent and marine protected areas from 11 to 20 percent by 2110. And South Africa, Mozambique, and Zimbabwe have joined forces in an exciting plan to create the world's largest animal reserve, a super park that would span three countries and allow animals to roam freely. In addition to nationally protected land, South Africa has about 9,000 privately owned game reserves.

Species at Risk

South Africa represents one percent of the Earth's land surface, but has almost ten percent of the world's known bird, fish, and plant species, and about six percent of its mammal and reptile species. But this natural wealth is under increasing threat because of the growing human population, loss of habitat for housing development and farming, illegal hunting for food, and illegal trade in wildlife and plants.

Species at risk include:

> African wild dog
> Barbour's rock mouse
> Black rhinoceros
> Blue swallow
> Botha's lark (bird)
> Bryde's whale
> Cheetah
> Freshwater sawfish
> Geometric tortoise
> Giant golden mole
> Major black millipede
> Mountain zebra
> Oribi (antelope)
> Pink velvet worm
> Pondoland
   cannibal snail
> Purcell's hunter slug
> Riverine rabbit
> Roseate tern (bird)
> Wattled crane
> Whistling rain frog
> Woodbush legless
   skink (reptile)

▼ A family of African wild dog puppies waits at the den for the adults to come back from a hunt.

Vegetation & Ecosystems Map

MAP KEY

Primary vegetation zones/ecosystems

- Deserts and dry shrublands
- Mangroves
- Mediterranean scrub
- Mountain grasslands
- Tropical and subtropical grasslands
- Tropical and subtropical moist broadleaf forests

Protected lands

- National parks

ZIMBABWE

MOZAMBIQUE

TROPIC OF CAPRICORN

Limpopo

BAOBAB TREE, page 21, AND BULL ELEPHANT, page 22

Kruger N.P.

Mapungubwe N.P.

SWAZILAND

RHINOCEROS, pages 2, 16–17

Richards Bay

Limpopo

BOTSWANA

KALAHARI DESERT

Marakele N.P.

WILD DOG PUPPIES, page 18

Pretoria (Tshwane)

Pilanesberg N.P.

AARDVARK, page 21

Johannesburg

Vaal

Golden Gate Highlands N.P.

Tugela

Indian Ocean

Durban

D R A K E N S B E R G

BLACK MAMBA, page 23

LESOTHO

East London

Orange

MEERKATS, page 20

Molopo

Bloemfontein

Great Fish

Sneeuberg

Suurberg N.P.

Port Elizabeth

Kgalagadi Transfrontier Park

Orange

Groot Vloer

Great Karoo

Camdeboo N.P.

Mountain Zebra N.P.

Addo Elephant N.P.

NAMIBIA

Augrabies Falls N.P.

Karoo N.P.

Little Karoo

Tsitsikamma Forest N.P.

Knysna

Wilderness N.P.

Richtersveld Transfrontier N.P.

MEADOW OF FLOWERS, page 24

Kamiesburg

Namaqua N.P.

Olifants

Tankwa Karoo N.P.

Hermanus

Cape Agulhas

Agulhas N.P.

PINK FLOWER, page 23

West Coast N.P.

Cape Town

Cape of Good Hope

Table Mountain N.P.

WHALES, page 25

Atlantic Ocean

miles 0 200

km 0 200

Life Among the Bushes

Veld is the Afrikaans word for a wild area of land. More than one-third of South Africa is covered by areas of grass and bushes, known as *bushveld*. The Kruger National Park protects a huge area of bushveld, and is one of the best places to see African wildlife. There are few hiding places for large animals, and many of the bushveld's animals, such as elephant, rhinoceros, and hippopotamus, are powerful creatures, so they can defend themselves from attack. Others, like zebra and antelope, rely on speed to stay out of danger. But even they have to remain on constant alert in order to flee from fast hunters such as lion and cheetah. The cheetah can reach speeds of 65 miles an hour (105 km/h) for a few seconds—just long enough to pounce on an unwary antelope, such as an impala or springbok.

▼ **Meerkats are nervous creatures. They spend a large amount of time standing on their hind legs looking around for danger.**

Desert Guards

Meerkats are small hunters that live in the dry areas of the Northern Cape. They have a different strategy for surviving in the veld. Bands of about 20 animals live in a network of burrows. While the rest of the band looks for food, the meerkats take turns standing sentry on a

THE UPSIDE-DOWN TREE

The African baobab is half as wide as it is high. Its immense trunk is filled with water so the tree can survive droughts. Hollows in the trunk provide homes for birds. Bats and bush babies (relatives of monkeys and lemurs) drink nectar from its flowers, baboons eat its fruit, and giraffes nibble its leaves. Humans also feed on the tree's seeds, fruits, and leaves. The fruit has six times more vitamins than an orange.

The baobab's strange trunk and thin rootlike branches have given rise to many legends. An Arabian story tells how the devil pulled the tree from the ground and planted it upside down. Because young baobabs look so different from the mature trees, a legend developed that the tree did not grow, but just arrived from the heavens. When it dies, the tree rots from within, and suddenly collapses into a heap of fibers, or again according to legend, they just disappear!

▲ Baobabs are among the longest-lived trees. Some are 5,000 years old.

mound or tree stump. They stand tall on their hind legs to get a better view and prop themselves up with their tails. If danger is sighted, the sentry gives a warning bark, and the meerkats flee to the safety of their burrows. If the threat is a snake, the adults huddle together and shoo it away.

Secretive Forest Dwellers

South Africa has very few forests. An exception is Knysna Forest on the coast of the Western Cape. Here giant yellowwood, stinkwood, and ironwood trees, ferns, lichens, and woody vines shelter colorful forest birds such as the Knysna loerie, the

▼ Aadvarks live all over South Africa. They have long snouts for rooting out ants and termites. *Aardvark* means "ant pig" in Afrikaans.

Cape parrot, and the rameron pigeon. Forest animals include the endangered samango monkey, bush pig, bushbuck, and blue duiker (a small antelope). The depths of the Kynsna forests are also home to a handful of very shy elephants, the last representatives of the huge herds that occupied the Cape region 400 years ago. These forest giants are so elusive that for many years scientists believed they had died out. Now they think that there may be just three or four living wild in the Cape. The last time one was spotted was in 2004.

Fields of Fire

The Cape is rather like a florist's store—only it is outdoors. An incredible number of plant species, including about 8,500 flowering species, are crowded into a small area. The Cape region covers less than one percent of Africa but contains nearly 20 percent of its plants. Table Mountain alone has more plant species than the whole of New Zealand! Some 70 percent of the Cape's plants grow nowhere else on Earth. In 2004 the United Nations opted to protect the flowers, and set up the Cape Floral Region. The reserve includes

▲ A bull elephant prepares to charge in the Kruger National Park. Despite bushveld being home to fierce hunters such as lions and leopards, and giants like elephants and rhinos, people are most likely to be killed by hippos.

Kirstenbosch Botanical Garden on the slopes of Table Mountain.

Fynbos—a type of shrubland that grows in the Cape—consists mainly of evergreen plants with small hard leaves, such as proteas and heathers. Many fynbos plants are burned down by the fires that are common during the dry summer months. The plants make the most of this. The intense heat of the fire causes seeds to sprout. The young plants use the ash from the fire as fertilizer. Others plants resprout from beneath fire-resistant bark or from underground bulbs.

The most famous of the fynbos flowers is the protea. The species was named after the Greek god Proteus, who could change his form at will. The name was chosen because the 330 species of protea have such different shapes, sizes, and colors.

Wind and Water

The semidesert area of the Northern Cape has very little rain. During summer the temperature is often higher than 104° F (40° C). Hot winds, called *bergs*, dry the land. Plants have to adapt to these extreme conditions. The most common

▲ The black mamba is the most dangerous snake in South Africa. Its bite can kill a person in 20 minutes.

▼ The petals of a king protea flower form the purple dome at the center. The border of pink points is formed by colored leaves, known as bracts.

DESERT BLOOMS

The seeds of about 4,000 species of plant lie beneath the sand and stones of Namaqualand, in the Northern Cape, waiting for rain. Sometimes they wait for years, but in some springs, when conditions are just right, the desert sands seem to explode in a frenzy of growth as flowers cover the land. White, red, and yellow daisies mingle with purple cineraria and blue flax. At the height of the season many other species also join the multicolored display. Only a small percentage of seeds germinate (sprout) each year, so if the initial rains do not continue, the plants still have a reserve for following years. During a good year plants produce huge quantities of seeds, which are scattered by the strong winds typical of the area. Different seeds germinate under different conditions of temperature and

▲ The flowers of Namaqualand attract many insects—and insect collectors.

moisture, which means that the flowers in each area differ from year to year, depending on when the first rains fall. So, although thousands of visitors come to see the flowers, it can be difficult to find the best locations and to get the timing right.

vegetation are succulent shrubs, which store water during the dry season in their fleshy leaves and stems.

Crowded Seas

South Africa's waters are rich in fish—about 2,000 species visit the coast at some point each year. One of the most spectacular fish events in the world is the Sardine Run. Every June a huge school of sardines arrives in the waters of KwaZulu Natal. The school is several miles long and contains millions of fish. The young fish have hatched out from their eggs near the Cape and are heading along the coast to warmer waters in the Indian Ocean. The sardines draw crowds of sharks, dolphins, birds, and people, all intent on catching them. As the fish are driven into shallow water by the dolphins and other hunters, people can scoop the fish up in buckets. Seabirds, such as gannets, sometimes eat so much that they cannot lift off the water, and are themselves eaten by sharks.

Water Monsters

South Africa's most awesome fish, and probably its most feared, is the great white shark. It has about 3,000 triangular teeth, arranged in several rows. The first two rows are used for grabbing and cutting prey, while the teeth in the rows behind replace front teeth when they are broken. Sharks do not chew food, they rip it into chunks and swallow it whole. People are rightfully scared of sharks, but in 2006 just four people died in shark attacks worldwide; more people are killed by dogs. In contrast millions of sharks are killed by people each year, and some species are now endangered.

POD PARTY

Every September the coastal town of Hermanus hosts a Whale Festival to celebrate the return of the southern right whales to the waters of Walker Bay. The arrival of whales off the shore is announced by the town's Whale Crier with the blow of a horn. Thousands of people create a human chain along the cliff path and join in the world's only Welcome Whales Wave. The three-day festival mixes whale watching with music and dancing.

Between June and November, southern right whales travel thousands of miles from the Antarctic to the shallow waters off the Cape to mate and give birth. The whale was given its name because whalers saw it as the "right" whale to hunt: It swam slowly and was easy to harpoon, and the body floated once it was dead. The whales' blubber, or fat, was boiled down to make oil for candles, cosmetics, and soap. In 1935 the right whale became a protected species, and its numbers are still slowly increasing.

▼ A southern right whale calf stays close to its mother in the waters of the Cape.

A Clash of Cultures

EVERY SEPTEMBER THOUSANDS of Zulus gather at KwaDukuza, on the coast north of Durban, to pay homage to their great king Shaka, who died there in 1828. The men wear traditional aprons—calf skin covers the rear, while a cat skin covers the front. They carry shields, spears, and short clubs called knobkerries. The women wear cowhide skirts and wide hats, all decorated with beads.

Poets sing the praises of all the Zulu kings, from Shaka to the present king, Zwelithini, who then gives a speech to his people. Cattle are slaughtered for feasting. The young women from each region try to outdance those from other regions. The young men have stick fights and show off to the women. The day is a celebration of the Zulu's power and history.

◀ **Zulu men dressed in traditional warrior clothing present themselves to their king during the King Shaka Day celebrations.**

CRADLE OF HUMANKIND

About 25 miles (40 km) from Johannesburg is a valley known as the Cradle of Humankind. It contains a maze of deep caves that have formed as underground water slowly washed away the rocks. The Sterkfontein Caves were discovered in 1896 by an Italian gold miner. Forty years later scientists found ancient bones of apelike humans, or hominids, in the caves. The bones were two million years old and had

gradually filled with minerals and turned into rocks called fossils. Since then scientists have found 500 hominid fossils, including a skeleton that may be four million years old, and many simple stone tools. These finds show that some of our earliest ancestors were living in the area. Burned animal bones, at least one million years old, show that these early humans cooked their food.

A walkway takes tourists over the site where some of the human fossils were found at the Sterkfontein Caves.

Time line

This chart shows the approximate dates for the population of South Africa from the arrival of early hunter-herders to its formation as a democratic republic.

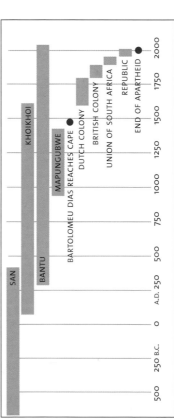

SAN
BANTU
KHOIKHOI
MAPUNGUBWE
BARTOLOMEU DIAS REACHES CAPE
DUTCH COLONY
BRITISH COLONY
UNION OF SOUTH AFRICA
REPUBLIC
END OF APARTHEID

500 B.C. 250 B.C. 0 A.D. 250 500 750 1000 1250 1500 1750 2000

Atlantic Ocean

TROPIC OF CAPRICORN

NAMIBIA

KALAHARI DESERT

BOTSWANA

ZIMBABWE

MOZAMBIQUE

Limpopo

Soutpansberg

Makapansgat

CERAMIC GIRAFFE, page 32

Mapungubwe Hill

SAN FAMILY, page 30

Lydenburg

Pretoria (Tshwane)

Swartkans

Kromdraai

Sterkfontein Caves

Johannesburg

FOSSIL CAVES, page 28

GOLD MINE, page 37

TOWNSHIP HOMES, page 41

Taung

Molopo

ododung

SWAZILAND

D R A K

Sharpeville Massacre, 1960

Battle of Blood River

SOUTH AFRICA

Vaal

BIG HOLE, page 38

BOER WAR SOLDIERS, page 39

Kimberley

Bloemfontein

Orange

Orange

LESOTHO

BATTLE OF BLOOD RIVER, page 37

WITCH DOCTOR, page 32

ZULU WARRIORS, pages 3, 26–27 AND ZULU PRINCE, page 35

Richards Bay

GRANARIES, page 31

Durban

Tugela

E N S B E R G

CAVE PAINTING, page 31

XHOSA VILLAGE, page 34

East London

Great Fish

Port Elizabeth

Grahamstown

Graaff-Reinet

Great Karoo

Little Karoo

Swellendam

HISTORIC HOUSE, page 36

STATUE, page 33

Cape Town

Cape of Good Hope

Indian Ocean

0   200
km

0   200
miles

MAP KEY

◆ Hominid sites

➤ Movement of Khoikhoi

➤ Movement of Bantu speakers

➤ Expansion of Trekboers, 1720–1770

□ Sites of interest

African kingdoms 1750's

Zulu

BaSotho

Swazi

BaPedi

• Selected present-day city

Present-day boundaries, drainage, and place names are shown.

The First South Africans

The earliest people to arrive in what is now South Africa were the San, or Bushmen, in about 22,000 B.C. The San roamed the countryside. They had no homes but built shelters from branches and grass when needed. They hunted with poison arrows, gathered fruit and honey, and dug up edible roots with sharpened sticks. They carried their water supply in ostrich-egg shells.

In about A.D. 100 a new people moved into the western and southern regions. They called themselves Khoikhoi, which means "men of men." The Khoikhoi were herders who moved from place to place to find fresh grasses for their animals. The Khoikhoi lifestyle

▼ A San man leads his children through the desert. The San have lived in Africa for 100,000 years. A few still live, much as their ancestors did, in and around the Kalahari Desert which stretches across northwest South Africa, Botswana, and Namibia.

PAINTED ROCKS

The San left a record of their lives in thousands of rock paintings throughout southern Africa. The richest collection is in the Drakensberg—about 20,000 paintings in 500 caves and overhangs. As invaders took over their lands, the San took refuge in these mountains. The artists made red, orange, yellow, black, and white paints from clays, burned wood, and minerals. They depicted animals, hunting scenes, and people. As they encountered European settlers the San also painted sailing ships, ox-wagons, and men with rifles. Historians believe that their paintings were not just decorative but had a powerful spiritual meaning.

▲ A cave painting in the Drakensberg shows a San hunter chasing a large antelope, probably an eland.

conflicted with that of the San, and the two groups often clashed over the centuries.

Farming Technology

Most modern-day South Africans are Bantu-speaking people. They moved south into the eastern regions of South Africa in A.D. 270. *Bantu* is the term for a set of languages. People with Bantu languages include the Shona, Ndebele, Basotho, Zulu, Xhosa, and Swazi.

Bantu also means "people," but the South African government misused the word in the 20th century as a label for all black people. The term is now seen as an insult and is not used in South Africa.

▼ A Zulu woman builds a granary using traditional techniques. The floor and walls are woven from grasses. Granaries like this have been used to store harvested crops in South Africa for more than 1,500 years.

▲ A Zulu *songoma*, or diviner, holds the head of a puff adder in his mouth. His skill with this deadly snake makes him a well respected and powerful member of the community.

The Bantu settlers spread new technology around South Africa: farming and ironworking. By about A.D. 400 most South African peoples were growing crops, such as millet, and were making metal tools. They also made masks from strips of clay and decorated them with glittering pieces of crystal. Many of these have been found near Lydenburg in northeastern South Africa. Historians think that the masks were used in rituals.

Stone Kingdom

From 1000 to 1300 Mapungubwe Hill, near South Africa's border with Zimbabwe, was the center of a prosperous kingdom. Its inhabitants, who were the ancestors of the Shona people, built drystone walls, which did not need cement, to create a complex system of stepped fields on the hill slopes.

The chief's relatives worked the best fields high on the slopes. Ordinary farmers, who lived at the bottom of the hill, grew millet, sorghum, and cotton, and kept cattle, sheep, and goats. Craftsmen made iron tools, copper pots, and gold jewelry. They also

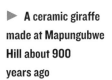

► A ceramic giraffe made at Mapungubwe Hill about 900 years ago

created ceramic figures and colored glass beads. The kingdom traded with cultures across Africa and Asia. People gradually left Mapungubwe and moved north into Zimbabwe, as the climate became drier.

Ships of Settlers

In the 1400s Portuguese sailors began exploring the coast of Africa as they looked for a sea route that would allow them to buy silks, spices, and other treasures from India and China. In 1488 Bartolomeu Dias rounded the Cape of Good Hope. Toward the end of the century Dutch and English ships began to stop in at Table Bay, just west of the Cape, to take on fresh water and trade goods with the Khoikhoi in exchange for food.

▶ A Xhosa village in the Eastern Cape is little changed since the Boers arrived in the 1800s.

▼ A young Xhosa man wears traditional face paint and headgear. The name Xhosa means "the fierce people."

The voyage between India and Holland could take about six months, and Dutch sailors wanted a place to resupply their ships on the way. In 1652, Dutchman Jan van Riebeeck established Cape Town close to Table Mountain to provide water, fruit, vegetables, and meat for passing ships. Van Riebeeck oversaw the planting of gardens and vineyards, which produced South Africa's first wine. He bought Khoikhoi cattle, paying for them with tobacco. However, it was not long before the Khoikhoi clashed with the Europeans, who then cleared the Africans from the area.

Expansion to the North

Some Dutch settlers came to Cape Town to farm the surrounding land. These Boers—Dutch for "farmer"—began to explore inland as they looked for more places to graze their cattle. These frontier farmers, or trek Boers, did not have ranches. They moved with their cattle in wagons. Most traveled east—the land to the west was too dry. Many Boers

SHAKA ATTACK

When Shaka became a chief of the Zulu people in 1815, he had served in the army of Dingiswayo, the supreme leader of a number of peoples, including the Zulus. Shaka immediately set about creating a powerful army. He shortened the Zulu spear, so it could be used to stab in hand-to-hand fighting instead of being thrown. If a Zulu warrior lost his spear it meant death, either in battle, or later as a punishment. Shaka organized soldiers into *amabutho,* or regiments, based on age. He also improved the traditional Zulu battle formation of a strong center, two fast moving "horns" that could encircle the enemy, and a reserve that could be sent wherever it was needed.

Dingiswayo died in 1816, and Shaka became the leader. He began to expand his empire. Within two years he had conquered a huge

▲ Zulu Prince Galenia, a descendent of King Shaka, wears leopard skins and carries a knobkerry at the annual gathering on King Shaka Day.

area—the present-day province of KwaZulu-Natal—and had an army of 40,000 men. In 1828 Shaka was killed by two half-brothers. One of them, Dingane, assumed power.

encountered Xhosa-speaking people living in the Eastern Cape. The two cultures immediately clashed, starting a long war for control of the land.

A British Colony

Far away in Europe, wars between the Netherlands and Britain led to the Cape Colony becoming British in 1806. The new British governor backed the Boers in their wars with the Xhosa, who were being violently driven from their land. In 1820, 5,000 British settlers arrived in the eastern Cape. They did not realize that they would be facing frequent raids by Xhosa soldiers and that the land was suitable for cattle but not for growing crops. Many gave up farming and settled in new towns like Port Elizabeth and Grahamstown.

Mass Movement

In the early 1800s two events had a huge effect on the peoples of South Africa. In 1816 the Zulu king Shaka took over most of the east of the country. And in 1834 slavery was made illegal in the Cape Colony. The Boers did not like the way this placed black Africans and ex-slaves from Asia on an equal footing with white Christians. They also disliked the increasing influence of the British in the colony. About 12,000 Boers—who now also called themselves Afrikaners—decided to move, or trek, north and east into what they wrongly believed was empty land ready for them to farm. This emigration was known as the Great Trek.

▼ The main house at the Vergelegen vineyard a few miles east of Cape Town was built in the early 1700s. The vineyard is one of the oldest in South Africa, and the house is built in the Dutch style of that time.

THE GREAT TREK

In the 1830s, the Boers living in the Cape Colony began to plan a way to escape British rule and start an independent Afrikaner state. Scouts found grassland all the way to the northern tip of the Drakensberg that was suitable land for settlement. The farmers secretly sold their properties and then set off in convoys of wagons. About 5,000 men, women, and children, called the Voortrekkers, meaning "pioneers," left the colony in the first two years, thousands more followed. Many died from disease, fights with African peoples, and accidents. Their hardships gave them a strong feeling of nationhood that resulted in the establishment of two Boer republics: the Orange Free State, in the center of present-day South Africa, and the South African Republic, or Transvaal, to the north.

▲ A painting of the Battle of Blood River of 1838, when trekkers fought the Zulus

By the mid-1800s white settlers lived on almost all of the land that was to become South Africa, with the exception of the Zulu kingdom and the mountain kingdom ruled by Moshoeshoe, which would become the nation of Lesotho.

▼ Miners work at a mine in the Cape in 1888. The work was hard and conditions were very dangerous.

Riches and War

In the 1860s diamonds were found in the bed of the Vaal River. In 1871 a rich new find brought diggers from all over the world. What had once been a hill became one of the biggest manmade holes in the world on the edge of a new town called Kimberley.

DIGGING FOR DIAMONDS

In 1867 a pretty pebble found by a child near the Orange River was identified as a diamond. Many more were found in what turned out to be one of the world's richest diamond mines. Four years later a new town, Kimberley, had sprung up to house the 30,000 miners who worked night and day digging for diamonds. When the diamonds ran out in 1914, the Big Hole, as the mine was called, was 2,600 feet (800 m) deep and had produced 3 tons (2.75 tonnes) of diamonds.

The family of farmers who had owned the land were the De Beers, and the De Beers Consolidated Mines was founded in their honor. The company controlled the number of diamonds being produced so that prices always remained high. By 1900 De Beers controlled about 90 percent of the world's supply of uncut, or rough, diamonds. De Beers is still the world's largest diamond company.

▲ The Big Hole mine, now flooded with years of rain, is just on the edge of present-day Kimberley.

In 1886 gold was found in Witwatersrand. It was not the first gold find in South Africa but it was the biggest strike. English-speaking miners flooded into the Transvaal. In just ten years the mining camp of Johannesburg had become a city of 100,000 people.

The discovery of such wealth had a vast impact on South Africa's history. Mining required huge numbers of laborers and new laws and taxes forced many Africans off their land and into the mines. In 1899 it also helped cause a war when British miners were blocked from working in Boer land. British forces came from across the British Empire, including Canada and India. They easily outnumbered the Boers, but their soldiers did not understand the country. The British wore bright red uniforms and were trained to fight in large battles. The Boer fighters were skilled horsemen and formed small mobile units called commandos, which harried the British and disrupted rail and supply lines. The British retaliated by burning farms and putting women and children in camps, where many died from disease. In 1902 the Boer War ended, and the Boers were forced to lay down their arms and accept British rule.

Forming a Union

The British now had four colonies in South Africa: the Cape, the Transvaal, the Orange Free State, and Natal —which was formed from the old Zulu kingdom. In 1910, the four were formed into an independent state

▼ Canadian troops try to keep out of sight as they slowly climb a kopje during the Boer War. This battle was the first time Canadian soldiers had fought abroad.

YOU HAVE STRUCK A ROCK

On August 9, 1956, about 20,000 women from all over South Africa and from all races marched on the city of Pretoria to protest against a law forcing black women to carry passes that would control where they lived and worked. Johannes Strijdom, the prime minister at the time, refused to meet with them. So, the protestors laid bundles of petitions with more than 100,000 signatures at his door. They ended by singing, "Now you have touched the women, Strijdom! You have struck a rock. You will be crushed!" Many of the women were arrested. The march marked the beginning of women's involvement in the struggle against apartheid. Their fight is remembered each year in the national holiday, Women's Day.

called the Union of South Africa. English and Afrikaans—a Dutch dialect spoken by Boers—became the two official languages. The new government soon began to bring in laws that separated whites and blacks. By 1936 only white South Africans were allowed to vote.

Divided Country

In 1948, the National Party won the general election. The party wanted to keep whites, especially Afrikaners, in charge of South Africa. In 1961, Prime Minister H. F. Verwoerd made South Africa a republic. The new republic practiced apartheid, meaning "separate development." This policy divided the black population into "nations," each with its own "homeland." Most South Africans and the rest of the world refused to recognize these areas as independent nations.

Millions of black Africans were forced to move into the homelands, which became overcrowded. Each black adult carried a pass which showed where they could live and work. A black person who could not show the correct pass when asked was arrested.

Marriage between different racial groups was forbidden, and all public institutions, offices, and transportation were racially segregated. The education system tried to keep black children at a very low standard so they could not be trained for skilled jobs.

Fighting for Freedom

Black people fought against their loss of freedom from the start. In 1912 the African National Congress (ANC) was founded. At first the ANC led nonviolent protests, but in 1960, 69 protesters were killed by police at Sharpeville. The ANC was banned and its leader, a Xhosa called Nelson Mandela, decided to use violence against the racist government. In 1963 Mandela was jailed for life for planning terrorist attacks.

The struggle continued in the 1970s and 1980s. Foreign countries stopped trading with South Africa. \In 1990 the new president F. W. de Klerk lifted the ban on the ANC and released political prisoners, including Mandela. In 1994, South Africa's first democratic election was held, and Nelson Mandela became the president of a black-dominated government.

▼ During the apartheid era, townships such as Soweto were sprawling slums, with shacks instead of properly constructed buildings.

The Rainbow Nation

MANY DIFFERENT PEOPLES make up South Africa's "rainbow nation," each with their own language, culture, and origins. The Ndebele (UHN-duh-beh-lay) live mainly in Northern and Mpumalanga provinces. The women decorate the walls of their mud houses with bold, geometric patterns every spring. The designs are passed down from mother to daughter. The women make paint brushes from bundled twigs and feathers and make paint from clay. The designs also appear on the women's shawls and elaborate beadwork jewelry. Traditionally, the patterns have a white background with red, blue, green, and orange designs on top. Modern designs include images of light bulbs, television aerials, and airplanes.

◀ An Ndebele woman stands in front of her newly painted house. She is wearing metal rings around her neck to show that she is married.

MOVING TO THE CITY

The map opposite shows that South Africa's most densely populated area is Gauteng where 20 percent of the country's population is crowded into just over 1 percent of its land. Unlike developing countries around the world, South Africa's people have not rushed to its cities; just under half continue to live in rural areas. This is not uncommon in Africa, where men leave their villages to find work in the cities but return home to their families regularly. Nevertheless, South Africa's cities are among the largest and most modern of any in the continent. Experts expect them to get larger still and forecast that by 2030, 71 percent of a population of 48 million people will be living in urban areas.

1950 / 13.5 million	1970 / 22.5 million
42% urban — 58% rural	47% urban — 53% rural

1990 / 37 million	2005 / 47.5 million
52% urban — 48% rural	59% urban — 41% rural

Common South African Phrases

With 11 official languages and scores of non-official African, Asian, and European languages there are many ways of saying "hello" in South Africa. Give them a try.

Afrikaans:	Goeiedag (Gweer dagg)
IsiNdebele:	Lotjhani (Lo tchar nee)
Sesotho:	Dumela (Doo meh lah)
Sotho:	Dumela (Doo meh lah)
Setswana:	Dumela (Doo meh lah)
SiSwati:	Sawubona (Sah woo bo nah)
IsiZulu:	Sawubona (Sah woo bo nah)
Xitsonga:	Avuxeni (Ah vuh cheh nee)
Tshivenda:	Ndaa (Uhn dah; to a male) / Aa (to a female)
IsiXhosa:	Molo (Moh low)

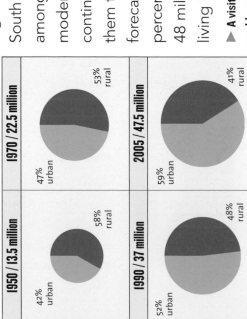

▶ A visit to a mall in **Johannesburg** is a world away from life in a traditional village.

Population Map

MAP KEY

People per square mile   **People per square kilometer**

Over 2500 — Over 1000

625–2499 — 250–999

62.5–624 — 25–249

12.5–62.4 — 5–24

2.5–12.4 — 1–4.9

Under 2.5 — Under 1

Population of urban area

□ Over 5 million

△ 1 million to 5 million

○ 500,000 to 1 million

• Under 500,000

ZIMBABWE

MOZAMBIQUE

TROPIC OF CAPRICORN

BOTSWANA

KALAHARI DESERT

NAMIBIA

SWAZILAND

LESOTHO

PAINTED WALL, pages 3, 42–43

Polokwane (Pietersburg)

SHOPPING MALL, page 44 AND SOCCER PLAYERS, page 49

Pretoria (Tshwane)

Witbank

Tembisa

Benoni

Boksburg

Vereeniging

Johannesburg

Krugersdorp

Brits

Soweto

Vanderbijlpark

Klerksdorp

Welkom

Virginia

Newcastle

Vryheid

Richards Bay

Pietermaritzburg

Durban

ZULU WOMAN WEARING HEADDRESS, page 47

D R A K E N S B E R G

BOY WITH TOY TRUCK, page 47

Bloemfontein

Botshabelo

Kimberley

East London

Bhisho

Port Elizabeth

Uitenhage

George

YVONNE CHAKA CHAKA, page 46 AND MINSTRELS, page 48

Paarl

Somerset West

Cape Town

Atlantic Ocean

Indian Ocean

miles   0   200

km   0   200

From Marabi to Kwaito

South Africans love music. Whether it is a social occasion, a church meeting, or a political rally, it will not be long before there is singing and dancing. The *toyi-toyi*, a defiant stomping dance combined with chanting, became world famous during South Africa's days of protest against apartheid.

In the 20th century the black townships produced South Africa's most exciting music. *Marabi* is lively jazzlike melodies played on a pedal organ. *Kwela*, meaning "get up" in Zulu, is played on a pennywhistle. *Mbaqanga* (um-ba-KON-ga) started out as African jazz but became the disco-style bubblegum music of the 1980s. In the 1990s *kwaito* swept the townships. Just as bubblegum had added a South African touch to

PRINCESS OF AFRICA

At age 16, in 1981, Yvonne Chaka Chaka (*right*) became the first black African child to appear on South African television. Her first album *I'm in Love With a DJ* sold 35,000 copies, and the title track became an instant hit. Chaka Chaka's music blended mbaqanga, a kind of jazz from the townships, with synthesizers to create a dance pop style that became known as bubblegum. Chaka Chaka's first album was followed by a string of hits through the 1980s and 1990s. Later she shed her disco image, began wearing African clothes, and was named the "Princess of Africa."

TOYS FROM TRASH

Nothing goes to waste in the townships of South Africa. Toys and trinkets are made from cans, wire, and even plastic grocery bags. At first they were made to entertain the township's children, but today works of art made from recycled material are exported around the world. There seems to be no end to the ingenuity of South African craftworkers: Flower vases made from the inner tube of a motorcycle tire; safety pin bracelets with "beads" made from telephone wire, computer cable scraps, and plastic tubing; paper maché bowls made from sardine can labels; colorful animals and birds made from plastic packaging; lunch boxes made from flattened soft drink cans; tote bags made from bottle tops and wire. Everywhere you go it seems that there is something new and original available from galleries, markets, and street vendors alike.

▲ A boy plays with a truck built from scrap metal. The boy steers with a wire sticking out of the top.

disco, kwaito gave a new sound to house music. In a country where nearly half the population is under 21, kwaito stars such as Bongo Maffin, Boom Shaka, and TKZee have huge followings.

▼ A Zulu woman wears an *isicolo*, a traditional headdress. Isicolos are made from hair woven over a frame.

Inventive and Colorful

South Africa has many artistic styles. Women wear colorful jewelry, including headdresses, necklaces, and bracelets made from beads. The patterns vary from district to district. Beadworkers produce ornaments and coverings for anything from a bottle of sauce to a matchbox. Traditional crafts, such as pottery and wood carving, have also been updated to appeal to modern shoppers.

NEW YEAR PARTY

Cape Town is South Africa's oldest city and is a mix of several cultures, including Khoikhoi, Indonesian, French, Dutch, British, and German. Half of Cape Town's residents are Coloreds (the name used for people of mixed race) with their own traditions.

On January 2 the city holds the biggest party of the year as the Colored community celebrates Tweede Nuewe Jaar (Second New Year). The festival was influenced by American minstrels on the cruise ships that called at the city in the 18th and 19th centuries. Thousands of minstrels with painted faces (*below*) take to the streets wearing bright satin uniforms and carrying colorful parasols as they sing and dance to toe-tapping banjo music.

Cookouts and Corn

A *braai* is the South African version of a barbecue. Most South African men pride themselves on getting their coals to just the right temperature and then providing huge plates of chops, *boerewors* (a spicy sausage), and *sosaties* (spicy mutton chunks on skewers).

South Africans also love the dried meat called *biltong*. No one knows who made the first biltong, which is a bit like beef jerky. African peoples dry strips of meat for using in stews, and the Dutch brought their own recipe for spicy dried meat from the Netherlands. Biltong—made from beef, venison, and ostrich—makes an ideal snack anywhere and anytime.

Corn has long been the basis for African cooking. You can buy roasted *mealies* (corn cobs) from stalls almost anywhere. Another favorite dish is *samp*—dried corn and beans. *Mielie-meal* (cornmeal), is used for everything from porridge to *mieliepap* (corn grits).

For something sweet South Africans enjoy preserves called

konfyt—melon or green figs cooked in syrup and spices—or *koeksusters*, fried dough coated in syrup.

United by Sports

South Africa is a sports-crazy nation, and sports are a way of building links between the nation's mix of peoples. Rugby was introduced to South Africa by the British and taken up by the Afrikaners. Black South Africans saw it as a white man's game and a symbol of segregation. In 1995 the national team, the Springboks, won the Rugby World Cup in Johannesburg. Nelson Mandela put on the shirt of the team's captain, a white Afrikaner. That gesture of reconciliation touched the nation.

But it is soccer that brings out the African crowds. Fans paint their faces and wear costumes in the local team's colors. In 2010 South Africa will be the first African nation to host the soccer World Cup.

South Africa is a leading cricket nation. The country is also home to world-class golfers, including Gary Player, Retief Goosen, and Ernie Els.

NATIONAL HOLIDAYS

Many of South Africa's holidays reflect its recent history. Human Rights Day commemorates the massacre at Sharpeville. Freedom Day celebrates the first democratic elections of 1994. Youth Day marks the 1976 protests by school pupils in Soweto that led to about 700 deaths. The Day of Reconciliation marks the Voortrekkers' Battle of Blood River with the Zulus in 1838, but now the holiday encourages national unity.

MARCH 21	Human Rights Day
APRIL 27	Freedom Day
MAY 1	Worker's Day
JUNE 16	Youth Day
AUGUST 9	Women's Day
DECEMBER 16	Day of Reconciliation
DECEMBER 26	Day of Goodwill

▼ Soccer is the most popular sport in South Africa, enjoyed by all of its people.

A New Republic

APRIL 27, 1994, WAS A DAY that many believed would never come—South Africa's first fully democratic election. Eager voters formed lines hours before the polls opened. In the countryside the lines snaked back and forth across fields, while in the cities they stretched for blocks. Young and old, black and white stood patiently together for hours. They shared food and used umbrellas to provide shade from the sun. Many black voters had dressed up in their best clothes to mark the importance of the day. Afterward people boasted about how long they had stood in line to vote as they celebrated. So many came that voting continued the next day. When the polls finally closed 87 percent of the country had turned out to elect South Africa's first black majority government.

◀ Supporters of the African National Congress (ANC), the largest political party in South Africa, celebrate the election of Nelson Mandela as the first president in 1994.

RESTRUCTURED COUNTRY

In 1994, the new government reorganized the administration of South Africa. It abolished the old provinces of Cape Province, Natal, Orange Free State, and Transvaal, as well as the areas that the apartheid government had made into "independent" homelands. It replaced them with nine smaller provinces. The provinces are divided into 52 districts, which are further divided into 231 local municipalities.

Each province has a government assembly. Between 30 and 80 members are elected for a five-year term, headed by a premier and an executive council. The size of the assembly is based on the number of voters living in the province. Provincial elections are held in the same year as the national elections. Each province sends delegates to the National Council of Provinces and recommends laws to the National Assembly.

▼ **Thabo Mbeki (*center*), the current South African president, greets San men during a meeting about land ownership.**

Trading Partners

South Africa's main exports are metals and minerals such as gold, diamonds, and platinum. The country's main imports are machinery and equipment, chemicals, and petroleum products. The countries of the European Union (EU) account for more than 40 percent of South Africa's imports and exports, but trade with Asian and Middle Eastern countries is becoming increasingly important.

Country	Percentage South Africa Exports
Japan	9.9%
United Kingdom	9.7%
United States	9.5%
Germany	6.5%
All others combined	64.4%

Country	Percentage South Africa Imports
Germany	14.2%
China	9.1%
United States	7.9%
Japan	6.8%
All others combined	62.0%

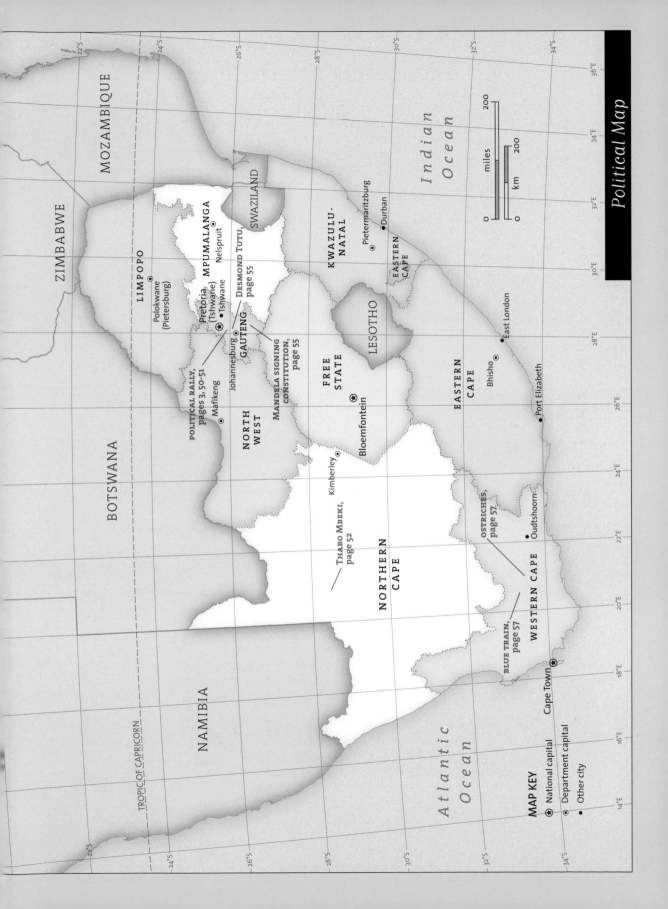

Political Map

MAP KEY
⊛ National capital
◉ Department capital
• Other city

Atlantic Ocean

Indian Ocean

NAMIBIA

BOTSWANA

ZIMBABWE

MOZAMBIQUE

ZIMBABWE

TROPIC OF CAPRICORN

NORTHERN CAPE

WESTERN CAPE

Cape Town ⊛

BLUE TRAIN, page 57

OSTRICHES, page 57

• Oudtshoorn

THABO MBEKI, page 52

• Port Elizabeth

EASTERN CAPE

Bhisho ◉

• East London

NORTH WEST

Kimberley ◉

POLITICAL RALLY, pages 3, 50–51

• Mafikeng

FREE STATE

Bloemfontein ⊛

LESOTHO

EASTERN CAPE

• Durban

Pietermaritzburg ◉

KWAZULU-NATAL

LIMPOPO

Polokwane (Pietersburg) ◉

Johannesburg ◉

GAUTENG

MANDELA SIGNING CONSTITUTION, page 55

Pretoria (Tshwane) ⊛
• Tshwane

MPUMALANGA

DESMOND TUTU, page 55

Nelspruit ◉

SWAZILAND

Scale
0 ___ 200 miles
0 ___ 200 km

Uncovering the Truth

After the 1994 elections, President Nelson Mandela faced the huge task of trying to right the wrongs of the apartheid era. He set up the Truth and Reconciliation Commission (TRC) and asked the country's leading churchman Desmond Tutu, Archbishop of Cape Town, to chair it. The TRC was like a court. Anybody who felt they had been a victim of human rights abuses between 1960 and 1994 could be heard. People who had committed the crimes could also explain what they did and ask to be forgiven. Over 20,000 people told their stories, many of which were broadcast on national television. In 1998, the Commission published

HOW THE GOVERNMENT WORKS

Every five years South Africans vote to elect members of the National Assembly. The National Assembly elects the president from among its members. The president appoints the Cabinet, the group of ministers that run the country. The laws created by the National Assembly are assessed and amended by the National Council of Provinces (NCOP). This body consists of 54 permanent members and 36 special delegates. Each of South Africa's provinces sends ten representatives to the NCOP—six permanent members and four special delegates. Judges are appointed by the president in consultation with the Judicial Service Commission and the leaders of political parties represented in the National Assembly.

GOVERNMENT

EXECUTIVE	LEGISLATIVE	JUDICIARY
PRESIDENT	NATIONAL ASSEMBLY (375 MEMBERS)	CONSTITUTIONAL COURT
CABINET (25 MINISTERS)	NATIONAL COUNCIL OF PROVINCES (90 MEMBERS)	SUPREME COURT OF APPEAL

Desmond Tutu wanted to be a teacher but frustration with the school system for blacks resulted in him becoming a minister. In 1984 Tutu won the Nobel Peace Prize for his nonviolent struggle against apartheid. In 1986 Tutu became Archbishop of Cape Town, the head of the South African church. He was the first black African to hold this post. Tutu retired to run the Truth and Reconciliation Commission. Despite the many terrible stories he heard, Tutu continued to counsel forgiveness rather than revenge.

▲ Desmond Tutu addresses township residents at the height of the struggle against apartheid.

a 3,500-page report, and presented it to Nelson Mandela. Mandela asked South Africans to accept the report and leave the past behind them as they work together to build a new country.

A New Constitution

South Africa's constitution is one of the most modern in the world. It gives all South Africans what many were denied during apartheid: equal rights to housing, healthcare, education, and justice. It also states that everyone has the right to use the language and participate in the culture of his or her choice. The constitution is unusually long, because it has deliberately been written in language that is easy to read and understand.

▼ Nelson Mandela signs the new South African constitution at Sharpeville in 1996. He chose Sharpeville for the signing because it was the site of one of the worst massacres of anti-apartheid protesters.

Mining Wealth

South Africa is the world's largest producer of gold, platinum, and chrome. It is also the world's fourth largest producer of diamonds. The Western Deep Level Gold Mine is 12,795 feet (3,900 m) deep—one of the deepest in the world. The rocks in the mine are warmed by the heat of Earth's core. The walls are warm to the touch. Giant air conditioners cool the air for the gold miners inside. Mining is dangerous. Earthquakes are common and can cause deadly rockfalls. Despite the dangers, men from all over southern Africa come to work in the mines.

A Few Farms

Only 13 percent of South Africa's land is suitable for growing crops, but farming is still important. Half of South Africa's water is used for agriculture. South Africa's chief exports are wine, fruits, sugar, and sunflower seeds.

One of South Africa's most unusual farm animals is the ostrich. In the 1800s

INDUSTRY MAP

This map shows the location of South Africa's industrial centers. The nation's manufacturing hub is Gauteng, which means "place of gold." As well as having gold mines and factories, this region is also the nation's center for financial and other service industries.

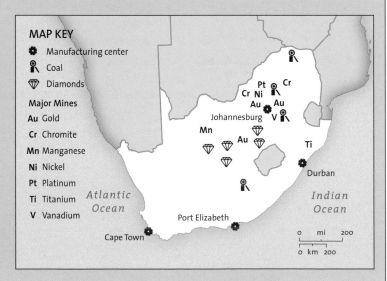

MAP KEY

- ❁ Manufacturing center
- ⚒ Coal
- ♦ Diamonds

Major Mines
- **Au** Gold
- **Cr** Chromite
- **Mn** Manganese
- **Ni** Nickel
- **Pt** Platinum
- **Ti** Titanium
- **V** Vanadium

Atlantic Ocean

Indian Ocean

Johannesburg

Durban

Port Elizabeth

Cape Town

0   mi   200
0   km   200

European women wore ostrich feathers in their hats and feather boas around their necks. The feathers came from immense ostrich farms in the Little Karoo. Feathers are no longer in great demand, but the giant birds are still bred for their meat.

Problems Solved

South Africans can be proud of the progress their country has made, but they still face challenges. There is a huge gap between rich and poor, and many people do not have jobs. For some, crime, such as robbery, is the only way to make a living. AIDS is also a huge problem. Five million people have the disease and many children have been orphaned.

However, there is still good news. During the times of apartheid, tourists would not visit South Africa as a protest against the racist system. Today, tourism is a growing industry as visitors are attracted to South Africa's sunshine, wildlife, and varied cultures.

TAKING THE BLUE TRAIN

In 1923 a distinctive sapphire-blue train began running between Johannesburg and Cape Town. People soon began referring to it as the "Blue Train," and the name has stuck. Since then presidents and kings have traveled in world-class luxury aboard the Blue Train. The 994-mile (1590 km) and 27-hour route crosses the Great Karoo, climbs through the Great Escarpment and passes through the highveld to Jo'berg (and now continues to Pretoria, too). Passengers have their own wood-paneled suites with marble bathrooms and enjoy meals in the dining car as the desert, mountains, or savanna pass by.

▲ The Blue Train stops at Matjiesfontein, a historic town in the Karoo.

▼ Ostriches can live in dry conditions, so they can be farmed in places that are unsuitable for cattle or sheep. Some ostrich farms allow tourists to take rides on the birds' backs.

Add a Little Extra to Your Country Report!

If you are assigned to write a report about South Africa, you'll want to include basic information about the country, of course. The Fast Facts chart on page 8 will give you a good start. The rest of the book will give you the details you need to create a full and up-to-date paper or PowerPoint presentation. But what can you do to make your report more fun than anyone else's? If you use your imagination and dig a bit deeper into some of the topics introduced in this book, you're sure to come up with information that will make your report unique!

>Flag

Perhaps you could explain the history of South Africa's flag, and the meanings of its colors and symbol. Go to **www.crwflags.com/fotw/flags** for more information.

>National Anthem

How about downloading South Africa's national anthem, and playing it for your class? At **www.nationalanthems.info** you'll find what you need, including the words to the anthem, plus sheet music for it. Simply pick "S" and then "South Africa" from the list on the left-hand side of the screen, and you're on your way.

>Time Difference

If you want to understand the time difference between South Africa and where you are, this Web site can help: **www.worldtimeserver.com**. Just pick "South Africa" from the list on the left. If you called someone in South Africa right now, would you wake them up from their sleep?

>Currency

Another Web site will convert your money into rands, the currency used in South Africa. You'll want to know how much money to bring if you're ever lucky enough to travel to South Africa: **www.xe.com/ucc**.

>Weather

Why not check the current weather in South Africa? It's easy—go to **www.weather.com** to find out if it's sunny or cloudy, warm or cold in South Africa right now! Pick "World" from the headings at the top of the page. Then search for South Africa. Click on any city. Be sure to click on the tabs below the weather report for Sunrise/Sunset information, Weather Watch, and Business Travel Outlook, too. Scroll down the page for the 36-hour Forecast and a satellite weather map. Compare your weather to the weather in the South African city you chose. Is this a good season, weather-wise, for a person to travel to South Africa?

>Miscellaneous

Still want more information? Simply go to National Geographic's World Atlas for Young Explorers site at **http://www.nationalgeographic.com/ kids-world-atlas/**. It will help you find maps, photos, music, games and other features that you can use to jazz up your report.

Glossary

Antelope a type of hoofed animal with horns that is related to cattle, sheep, and goats. Antelopes live in Africa and Asia only. They include wildebeests, waterbucks, and oryxs.

Ceramic a material made from shaping or molding clay and then heating it in an oven. Pottery is a type of ceramic.

Climate the average weather of a certain place at different times of year.

Colony a region that is ruled by a nation located somewhere else in the world. Settlers from that distant country take the land from the region's original inhabitants.

Diviner a medicine man, or witch doctor.

Economy the system by which a country creates wealth through making and trading in products.

Ecosystem a community of living things and the environment they interact with; an ecosystem includes plants, animals, soil, water, and air.

Edible something that can be eaten.

Empire territories located in several parts of the world that are controlled by a single nation.

Escarpment a cliff-like feature in the landscape where an area of high and flat land meets an area of low-lying land.

Fertile good for growing plants and supporting life.

Financial relating to finance, the management of money by companies, governments, and individuals.

Fossil a body part or other piece of evidence left by a living thing that is preserved in rock.

Geometric a pattern or structure that is made up of regular shapes.

Germinate the process by which a seed grows tiny roots and a stem to form the first parts of a plant.

Habitat a part of the environment that is suitable for certain plants and animals.

Latitude an imaginary straight line that circles the Earth connecting points of land that are all the same distance from the Equator. The Equator has a latitude of 0 degrees (0°).

Marine describing something that is linked to the ocean.

Mineral a chemical that is found naturally in the environment.

Natural resources naturally occurring materials and substances that can be collected and sold. Natural resources include oil, metals, or lumber.

Nectar the sugary liquid produced by some flowers to attract insects and other animals to them.

Petition a document asking the government to change a law or policy. Most petitions are signed by many hundreds or thousands of people to ensure that lawmakers take notice.

Recycle to use an item or material again for a purpose different from its original use.

Species a type of organism; animals or plants in the same species look similar and can only breed successfully among themselves.

United Nations (UN) an international organization that includes most of the countries of the world. The UN is where governments discuss the world's problems and figure out how to work together to solve them.

Bibliography

Hamilton, Janice. *South Africa in Pictures*. Minneapolis, MN: Lerner Publications, 2004.

Kramer, Ann. Mandela: The Rebel Who Led His Nation to Freedom. Washington, D.C.: National Geographic, 2005.

Mulla-Feroze, Umaima. *Welcome to South Africa*. Milwaukee, WI: Gareth Stevens Pub., 2003.

Murphy, Patricia J. *South Africa*. New York, NY: Benchmark Books, 2004.

http://news.bbc.co.uk/1/hi/

world/africa/country_profiles/1071886.stm (general information)

http://www.gov.za/ (official Web site of the South African government)

http://www.southafrica.info/ (general information)

Further Information

NATIONAL GEOGRAPHIC Articles

"Africa's New Eye on the Sky." NATIONAL GEOGRAPHIC (July 2006): Space.

Godwin, Peter. "City of Hope, City of Fear: Johannesburg." NATIONAL GEOGRAPHIC (April 2004): 58–77.

Web sites to explore

More fast facts about South Africa, from the CIA (Central Intelligence Agency): https://www.cia.gov/cia/publications/factbook/geos/sf.html

The Zulu are the largest cultural group in South Africa with a long and proud history. Find out more about them by looking at this site: http://zululand.kzn.org.za/zululand/index.html

Nelson Mandela is the most famous South African in the world. Find out more about him at http://news.bbc.co.uk/1/hi/world/africa/1454208.stm

See, hear

There are many ways to get a taste of life in South Africa, such as movies, music, magazines, or TV shows. You might be able to locate these:

Cry Freedom (1987)
A movie set in South Africa during the 1970s. The story is based on Steve Biko, a leader of the campaign against apartheid. Biko was played by Denzel Washington in his first major movie performance.

The Gods Must Be Crazy (1980)
A comedy set in the Kalahari Desert with a San bushman taking the lead role. The story relates what happens after a bottle of soda is dropped from an airplane into a San camp. The San have never seen a bottle before and its arrival changes their world forever.

Ladysmith Black Mambazo
This male-voice choir from Ladysmith, KwaZulu-Natal, is among the most famous of South Africa's musical groups. Their musical style, in which they sing largely unaccompanied by instruments, is one of the most recognizable of all forms of South African music.

J. M. Coetzee
South Africa's greatest living author, J. M. Coetzee has won many awards for his books, including the Nobel Prize for literature in 2003. His most famous book is *Disgrace*.

Index

Credits

Picture Credits

NGIC = National Geographic Image Collection
Front Cover – Spine: Stacy Gold/NGIC; Top: Chris Johns/NGIC; Low Far Left: Paul Sutherland/NGIC; Low Left: Ralph Lee Hopkins/NGIC; Low Right: Tomasx Tomaszewski/NGIC; Low Far Right: Tomasz Tomaszewski/NGIC.

Interior – Corbis: O. Alamany & E. Vicens: 21 up; Bettmann 37 lo; Wayne Conradie/epa: 46 lo; Roger De La Harpe: 32 lo; Roger De La Harpe/Gallo Images: p35 up; Peter Guttman: 3 left, 42-43; Hulton-Deutsch Collection: p39 lo; Bob Krist: 57 center; Charles O' Rear: 14 up, 55 lo; Philip Richardson: 38 up; David Turnley: 3 right, 50-51, 55 up; K. M. Westermann: 33 up; NGIC: James P. Blair: 2 left, 6-7, 31 lo, 34 lo; Jonathan Blair: 11 up, 23 lo, 24 up; Nicole Duplaix: 2 right, 16-17, 30 lo; Kenneth Garrett: 28 up, 57 lo; Stacy Gold: 11 lo, 12 lo, 36 lo; George Grall 23 up; Bobby Haas: 25 lo; Chris Johns: 5 up, 22 center, 31 up, 32 up, 52 lo; Ed Kashi: 47 lo; Mattias Klum: 20 center; Frans Lanting: 21 lo; Walter Maeyers Edwards: p34 up, 37 up; Steve McCurry: 15 up, 48 lo; W. A. Rogers: 2-3, 10 up, 26-27, Jame L. Stanfield 13 lo; Tomasz Tomaszewski: 15 lo, 41 lo, 44 up, 47 up, 49 lo; Volkmar K. Wentzel: TP; Kim Wolhuter: 18 center; Shutterstock: Mark Atkins: 59 up.

For more information, please call 1-800-NGS-LINE (647-5463) or write to the following address:

NATIONAL GEOGRAPHIC SOCIETY
1145 17th Street N.W.
Washington, D.C. 20036-4688 U.S.A.

Visit the Society's Web site at
www.nationalgeographic.com/books

Library of Congress Cataloging-in-Publication Data available on request
ISBN: 978-1-4263-0203-9

Printed in the United States of America

Series design by Jim Hiscott.
The body text is set in Avenir; Knockout.
The display text is set in Matrix Script.

Front Cover—Top: San children playing in the desert; Low Far Left: Tribal beaded bracelets on sale; Low Left: A jackass penguin on a beach at sunrise; Low Right: Schoolgirls prepare to perform at a store opening; Low Far Right: Street scene, Johannesburg

Page 1—Female members of the Zulu royal family wearing traditional beaded jewelry gather for a wedding; Icon image on spine, Contents page, and throughout: Zebra stripes

Produced through the worldwide resources of the National Geographic Society

John M. Fahey, Jr., *President and Chief Executive Officer*; Gilbert M. Grosvenor, *Chairman of the Board*; Nina D. Hoffman, *Executive Vice President, President of Book Publishing Group*

National Geographic Staff for this Book

Nancy Laties Feresten, *Vice President, Editor-in-Chief of Children's Books*
Bea Jackson, *Director of Design and Illustration*
Jim Hiscott, *Art Director*
Virginia Koeth, *Project Editor*
Lori Epstein, *Illustrations Editor*
Stacy Gold, Nadia Hughes, *Illustrations Research Editors*
Priyanka Lamichhane, *Assistant Editor*
R. Gary Colbert, *Production Director*
Lewis R. Bassford, *Production Manager*
Maryclare Tracy, Nicole Elliott, *Manufacturing Managers*
Maps, *Mapping Specialists, Ltd.*

Brown Reference Group plc. Staff for this Book

Volume Editor: Tom Jackson
Designer: Dave Allen
Picture Manager: Clare Newman
Maps: Martin Darlison, Encompass Graphics
Artwork: Darren Awuah
Index: Kay Ollerenshaw
Senior Managing Editor: Tim Cooke
Design Manager: Sarah Williams
Children's Publisher: Anne O'Daly
Editorial Director: Lindsey Lowe

About the Author

VIRGINIA MACE is an honors graduate of Rhodes University, South Africa. She has worked in illustrated book publishing for more than 20 years as an editor and author both in South Africa and the United Kingdom. She lived in South Africa for 17 years and returns on regular visits.

About the Consultants

KATE ROWNTREE is a professor of geography at Rhodes University in South Africa. Her research focus is geomorphology and catchment management. She has led a number of research projects on these topics in South Africa, where she has lived since 1985. She is coeditor of the textbook *The Geography of South Africa in a Changing World* (OUP 2000) and has published widely on her South African research.

DR. VUKILE KHUMALO teaches African History in the School of Anthropology, Gender and Historical Studies at the University of KwaZulu-Natal. He has published journal articles and chapters on cultural history, political economy, and political imagination in 19th-century South Africa. His current research is on public sphere and public violence before the formation of the Union of South Africa in 1910.

Time Line of
South African History

B.C.

ca 22,000 San people begin to settle the region of South Africa.

A.D.

ca 270 Bantu-speakers settle south of the Limpopo River in an area occupied by Khoikhoi and San for thousands of years. The Bantu introduce ironworking to the region.

ca 1000 Mapungubwe Hill is the center of a prosperous kingdom.

1400

1400s Zulu and Xhosa peoples establish large kingdoms in southern Africa.

1488 Portuguese explorers sail around the Cape of Good Hope; the cape becomes a regular stop-off on sea journeys to Asia.

1600

1652 The Dutch East India Company founds the Cape Colony and establishes the port of Cape Town.

1800

1806 Cape Colony becomes British as a result of wars fought in Europe.

1815 Shaka becomes king of the Zulu.

1834 The British make slavery illegal in Cape Colony, angering Boer settlers.

1836 Boer settlers move north to escape increasing British control and found the Orange Free State and Transvaal. This two-year overland migration, the "Great Trek," becomes a central event in Boer history.

1856 Encouraged by a prophetess who claims to convey their ancestors' commands, the Xhosa kill all their cattle and are devastated by the destruction of their economy.

1867 Diamonds are discovered in Kimberley, attracting foreign settlers, investment, and development to Cape Colony.

1879 British troops take control of Natal after a six-month war against the Zulu.

1880 Boers rebel against the British, beginning the year-long Anglo-Boer War.

1886 The discovery of gold at Witwatersrand sparks a gold rush.

1899 The second Anglo-Boer War starts when British troops gather on the Transvaal border.

1900

1902 The Treaty of Vereeniging ends the second Anglo-Boer War and makes the Transvaal and Orange Free State self-governing British colonies.

1910 The Cape, Natal, Transvaal, and Orange Free State join to form the Union of South Africa.

1912 The Native National Congress is founded to protect the rights of black South Africans; it is later renamed the African National Congress (ANC).

1913 The Land Act prevents most blacks from buying land outside reserves.